Religions
East and West

By the Same Author

Dreams
Drums, Rattles, and Bells
Flutes, Whistles, and Reeds
Gliders
Haunted Houses
Horns
Investigating UFO's
Kites
Magic Made Easy
The Magic of Sound
Puzzle Patterns
Shadows
Singing Strings
Sixth Sense
Song, Speech, and Ventriloquism
Spinning Tops
Spooky Magic

Larry Kettelkamp

RELIGIONS
EAST AND WEST

William Morrow and Company
New York 1972

Kettelkamp, Larry.
  Religions, East and West.

  SUMMARY: Discusses the similarities and differences
of ten of the world's major religions.
  1. Religions—Juvenile literature. [1. Religions]
I. Title.
BL92.K45   200'.9   72-75805
ISBN 0-688-20030-3
ISBN 0-688-30030-8 (lib. bdg.)

Contents

Preface

Viewpoints on early religions constantly are being revised and are partly a matter of opinion. Where there are conflicting views, the author has tried to present opposing ideas objectively. Although there often is no clear dividing line between fact and legend, distinctions have been made wherever possible.

Today students of religion are concerned with prophetic insight along with traditional scholarship. Such sources as the trance readings of the late Edgar Cayce are being given limited scholarly attention, since they provide a wealth of detail relating to religious history. Accordingly, the author has included some of the Cayce material, particularly where it agrees with at least one current of traditional opinion. In the listing of the questions of Osiris, the author has compromised between those found in versions of the Egyptian *Book of the Dead* and those in *Winged Pharoah* by the trance psychic, Joan Grant.

The view that developed cultures once existed on ancient island continents is not currently popular among many scholars. Although it conflicts with the commonly held version of world history, however, there is limited concrete evidence along with material from prophetic sources to support this belief. The author feels that future finds may bear out this thinking and so has drawn his material from both traditional and nontraditional sources in order to present this overview of the world's religions.

The author wishes to thank Professor Benjamin Ray, Historian of Religions, Princeton University, for offering helpful suggestions and providing valuable source material. Views and opinions expressed in the book are, of course, those of the author.

Larry Kettelkamp
Cranbury, New Jersey, 1972

Introduction

Everyone has some beliefs that cannot be proved. One cannot be certain that the sun will rise tomorrow, but most people believe that it will. One could not live with confidence from day to day if he did not trust that certain laws would hold true. Such faith is the basis of religion.

At first the word *religion* meant *awe of the gods.* It was used to refer to powers both outside oneself and within as well. These powers influenced a person's choices and actions. Today religion might be defined, in its broadest sense, as the search for the values of an ideal life. However and wherever they began, the world's religions have tried to answer questions people have about their identity and to point the way to ideal living.

Among the principal religions there are many differences, but at the same time there are certain ideas that they all share. Each religion seems a piece of a giant puzzle in which the whole is greater than the parts. Yet the parts are not separate. Ideas are passed on, and rules are borrowed and shared. Also, a kind of alternation seems to occur. Beliefs stressed by one religion may be passed over by another. For example, the quiet philosophies and mental disciplines of the countries of the Far East stand in contrast to the activist practices in many of the countries in Europe, Africa, and the Americas.

Recently there has been a rediscovery of Eastern religions in the West. This blending of Eastern and Western philosophies has brought about basic changes in religious thought today. People no longer ask which views are right or wrong, but feel that all beliefs are important and should be considered together.

In addition, current research is suggesting fresh theories about the beginnings of man's religions. Archeologists are finding new links among different cultures of the past. Legends of what were once thought to be mythical lost continents are now being seriously considered, and these stories suggest that various religions had a common source in the distant past.

Today the studies of modern science are overlapping with those of religion in the search for that part of man which seems eternal and hidden. New theories about the mind, the soul, and life after death are being discussed. Scientists and religious teachers are coming to realize that their disciplines have much to offer each other.

Here is the story of how the world's principal religions originated, who the religious leaders were, and what work is being done today that will influence the faith of the future.

Part I
RELIGIONS
OF THE
EAST

Osiris, Egypt, and the Sun King

In a monastery in the Himalayan mountains of Tibet is an ancient tablet telling of the life of a religious leader named Osiris. In another monastery in India is a second tablet with a similar inscription.

According to the legends on these tablets, Osiris grew up in Atlantis, a continent that once was located in the Atlantic Ocean thousands of years ago. As a young man Osiris traveled to Lemuria, another continent then in the South Pacific Ocean. There he entered a college, studying religion and science.

He became what was called a master and returned
to Atlantis. In his own country people were skilled
in medicine and science and the use of the mind.
But social problems existed, because many people
were too selfish and too proud of their own accom-
plishments. So Osiris became a religious teacher
and reformed the ways of his countrymen.

Egyptian God, Osiris, holding scepter
and harvest flail. Throne is an ancient
shape meaning *builder*. At right, the
lotus, symbol of plant life.

As the chief priest in Atlantis, Osiris grew so popular that the people wanted to force King Ouranos from his throne and put Osiris in his place. Although Osiris refused, other leaders were nevertheless jealous of his popularity. Thus, after many years, Osiris was murdered by one of his own brothers.

After his death Osiris was considered a god, and a religion grew up around his teachings. The son of Osiris was named Horus, and he became the chief priest in Atlantis. Accordingly, the name Horus was used to designate those who followed him as the head of the Osirian church.

An old Egyptian legend tells the story of a man named Thoth, who was the son of a priest in Atlantis. Before the final destruction of Atlantis, he brought a group of people to northern Egypt on the Nile River and founded a colony there. The name of the town was Sais, and in it Thoth built a temple and spread the teachings of the Osirian religion. Religious leaders, also given the title of Horus, ruled the Egyptian colony from the time of Thoth down to the time of the ruler Menes.

Eventually Horus and Thoth were called gods

too. Soon many other gods were added to the list.
The god Ptah symbolized creative power, and Set,
the brother who was said to have murdered Osiris,
was called god of death. Hathor, or Isis, was the
female symbol of nature and the sister-wife of
Osiris. Bast was the wife of Ptah, and they had a
son named Atum. In addition, some of the ancient
gods representing the sun were worshiped in special
cities and towns. The sun god, Re, was one of them.

Actually there are many different legends about
Osiris and the other Egyptian gods. Some historians
feel that Osiris probably never lived. But however
it began, the religion of Osiris became an important
part of Egyptian life. Considered the god of the
afterworld, Osiris was associated with the earth and
growing plants and the idea of resurrection. This
concept may have developed from the flooding of
the Nile River each year, which brought water for
fresh crops.

However, the priests of the sun gods and those of
Osiris came to oppose each other. A city called
Heliopolis, which means *sun city,* grew up in northern Egypt. The priests of Heliopolis combined the
religion of Osiris with their own teachings about

the sun. Horus, the son of Osiris, became known as the sun god. The Egyptian kings were believed to be gods too, either Horus himself or another important deity in human form.

In the teachings of the Osirian religion there was a list of forty-two questions that gave the goals of the spiritual life. At the time of death, each person was to account for himself by answering the questions as to how he had lived his life on earth. Many variations of this list have been found, but usually it contains most of those principles that were stated later in the ten commands of Moses. Similar rules have appeared in many other religions.

Here are a few examples of one version of the forty-two Osirian questions:

Have you treated your body wisely?

Have you been thankful for all that has touched you in time of need?

Have you given bread and wine to the poor and the weary?

Have you taken nothing from another which was not yours?

Have you honored your father and your mother?

Have you spoken that truth which you have for the
benefit of others?

Have you remembered the messengers of God and
asked their counsel?

Have you killed no man in violence?

Have you seen the best self that is in you?

Have you helped all upon earth as fellow travelers on
the great journey?

Many of these beliefs remained much the same
until Amenhotep the Fourth became ruler of Egypt
about 1386 B.C. He married his own sister, Nefertiti, whose name means "the beautiful one is come."
Together he and his sister-wife drastically reformed
the Egyptian religion. The new king opposed the
idea of local gods acclaimed by priests in various
cities. He was a poet, artist, and philosopher. Ignoring the military problems of the country, he concentrated on religious concerns. He chose the Aton,
a symbol of the sun's disc, as the religious symbol
of his country. It represented the universal creator
of all things in all lands. The sun itself was not to
be worshiped, but represented the source of all life.

Amenhotep also changed his name to Ikhnaton,

Realistic sculptures of the
sun king, Ikhnaton, and
his sister-queen, Nefertiti.

he who satisfies Aton. He left the capital city at
Thebes with a small band of devoted priests to
found a new city about twenty miles north on the
Nile River. The city was called Akhetaton, *horizon
of Aton.* The buildings were simply but artistically
constructed; temples had roofs open to the sun.
Paintings and statues were made more lifelike in
the spirit of Ikhnaton's search for the one truth.

Ikhnaton's sun disc was drawn or carved with
rays extending beneath it. At the end of each ray
an open hand was pictured, blessing the land and

Ikhnaton's sun symbol
of the creator, hands
reaching down in blessing.
Looped cross is Egyptian
sign of life.

the people. Statues and busts of Ikhnaton and Nefertiti, which are amazingly realistic and show the couple much as they must have looked, have been unearthed and preserved.

A hymn to the Aton, written by the king himself, was found carved on the wall of a tomb chapel. Here is a translation of part of the poem:

You appear beautifully on the horizon of heaven,
O living Aton, beginning of life!
When you have risen in the East,
You have filled every land with your great beauty.

Gracious you are, great, glistening, high over the earth.
Your rays span the lands to the limits of all you have
    made.
As you are the source point, so you reach even to the
    end points of your rays.
Though far away, your rays are on earth;
Though you are in their faces, no one knows your
    works.

All beasts are content in their places;
Trees and plants flourish.
Even birds from their nests
Stretch forth their wings in praise to your creation.

You bring forth the Nile at your desire
To maintain the people of Egypt.
Even as you have made all people and are lord over all,

So are you lord of every land, rising for all,
Aton of the day,
Great in majesty.

The beauty and simplicity of Ikhnaton's religion
did not last. After his death the worship of many
gods revived more strongly than ever. In thirty years
the temples in the new capital city were destroyed,
and the name Ikhnaton was chiseled out of the
inscriptions on the monuments. However, some of
the universal spirit of the Aton was given later to
the old god Amon. Furthermore, the theme of Ikhnaton's religion of one god, a universal creator,
remains long after the city gods of Egypt have
passed from history.

Hinduism and Buddhism

Elsewhere in the East other religions were established. According to tradition, holy men from the Far East, called Na-acals, brought their teachings to the subcontinent of Asia that is India today. A people called the Nagas settled there, thousands of years ago, and much later a people called the Aryans invaded the land.

The fair-skinned Aryans considered themselves superior to the darker-skinned Nagas, and their beliefs gave rise to India's caste system. Accord-

ingly, a person's status in society became determined
by his color or his occupation. People married only
those of the same class, and their children also
belonged to that particular caste group. Priests
formed the highest class, warriors and rulers the
second, merchants and landowners the third, and
the serfs the lowest. Those who did the most un-
sanitary tasks later made up still another group, the
"out-castes" called untouchables.

India became a melting pot of religious ideas.
Over the centuries the writings and beliefs of its
various people developed into the Hindu religion.
The name of the religion, like the name of the
country, comes from the Indus River.

The basis of Hinduism is the sacred literature
called the Vedas, a word that means *spiritual wisdom*. The Vedas are collections of hymns, or chants,
sacrificial rites, and philosophical reflections. Some
of the selections are much like the psalms of the
Old Testament. The last of the books included in
the Vedas contains approximately one hundred po-
ems about the search for meaning in life and is
called Upanishads, meaning *sitting near in devotion*.
Much later an epic poem called the Bhagavad Gita,

or *Song of God,* expressed the spirit of popular Hinduism. It is often called the Hindu bible.

The Bhagavad Gita tells of a struggling disciple named Arjuna, whose life is filled with problems. At one point he must decide whether or not to lead a military battle in which some of his relatives are in the enemy camp. The god, Krishna, who answers Arjuna's questions, replies that the young warrior must follow the duty of his military caste. Krishna explains that although death in battle is tragic, a man's eternal soul cannot be taken from him by this misfortune or any other.

The main theme running through the Hindu religion is that of detachment. This idea is difficult to understand. The Hindu feels that men strive toward four basic goals in life. The first goal is pleasure; the second is success. For many, these are of prime importance. Those who tire of pleasure and success, however, may choose a third goal, that of service to others. These people undertake much community work. Nevertheless, men eventually find that none of these three goals bring complete happiness. The world is still full of problems; something still seems to be missing. Then the searcher turns to the last goal, that of detachment. Although his life is full of joys and sorrows, he passes beyond them.

Detachment does not mean withdrawal from life. Instead, this concept is intended to free a person, even from the results of his efforts. The man who is detached works to the best of his ability, serves to the best of his ability, and thinks to the best of his ability. Failure does not deter him, for he cannot be disappointed. Great success, when it comes, does not inflate him with false pride. He lives and acts to his fullest potential.

The Hindu describes this freedom with several terms. One is Brahma. Brahma represents a creator who cannot be understood or described. Although Hindus worship many lesser gods and depict some of them as human figures, they believe that each represents a quality of one god, the one source. When a person comes to know them, he understands the different aspects of god at work in the universe.

Another Hindu idea is that of Nirvana. Like Brahma, it cannot be understood. It is a state of being that has no beginning or end; it is timeless, without form. Nirvana is both a loss of all that is apart from God and a union with life everywhere. Nirvana is that toward which the Hindu always is striving. Yet it is that which is always present.

One of the strongest Hindu beliefs is that of Karma, which means simply *deed*. It is the same as the principle of modern science that states that every action creates a reaction. As a man acts toward others, so will they act toward him. What each one does eventually returns to him in kind. To a Christian, the idea usually takes the form of reward and punishment; a man may be judged for his actions in an afterlife. To the Hindu, man is constantly responsible for his own behavior and reaction to it takes place automatically.

Hindus are taught that life on earth is a giant wheel. Each soul lives a series of lives, thus gaining total experience. If a person has been helpful to other people in one lifetime, these same people, in different bodies, tend to return the kindness in a later lifetime. Similarly a person who does violence in one lifetime will meet with violence himself in another lifetime. In this way each personality or soul has a chance to find out in another life how one feels when he is treated as he has treated others.

During a single lifetime there are many seeming injustices. One person may be a beggar, one a prisoner, one a king, one a saint. One person may live a short life and another a long one. However, because Karma is at work in the universe, the situations may be reversed in following lifetimes. If a person is aware of this pattern and constantly tries to be helpful, at last he can leave the earth and move toward Nirvana, or union with God.

The belief in reincarnation became linked with the concept of the caste system. To Westerners, the idea of being born into a certain level of society that cannot be changed seems unjust. Since the Hindu expects to live many lifetimes, however, he feels that the man who is a serf at one time may earn the chance to be a king at another. A rich merchant who misuses his money may be born later as a beggar. To the Hindu, one lifetime is a tiny portion of the whole. Recently, however, modern reformers, such as Gandhi, and the influences of Western cultures have made the rigid caste system more flexible. Today education and training rather than birth may determine the opportunities open to many people.

Interestingly, the principle of rebirth was not original with the Hindus. It was a part of most ancient religions in some form. For example, an early Egyptian papyrus by Anana, dated about 1320 B.C., states:

> Man comes into being many times, yet knows nothing of his past lives except, occasionally, some daydream or thought carries him back to a circumstance of a previous incarnation. . . . In the end, however, all of his past lives will reveal themselves.

One element of Hinduism recently has become popular in the United States and other Western countries. It is the practice of Yoga, which is the Indian word for *yoke.* According to this belief, a person may gain enlightenment through any of four disciplines, each suited to a different personality. First is the Yoga of knowledge, the intellectual path to self-understanding; second is the Yoga of love, the selfless relationship with all people and all things; third is the Yoga of action, the doing of deeds that are worthy; fourth is the Yoga of direct experience, the finding of one's self through meditation.

The last of the four Yogas combines control of the body through exercise and posture with control of the mind through concentration and meditation. Westerners have discovered that the practice of Yoga can be an excellent way to relieve the tensions caused by the frantic and confusing pace of modern living. Yoga taught by qualified instructors is now available almost everywhere, even on television.

Yoga begins with exercises to limber the body and to improve circulation. Most important is a special crossed-legged sitting position called the "lotus." Beginners do not need to achieve the complete position, but are taught gradual steps leading to it. In the lotus position, the back is held straight even though the person feels relaxed. Yoga is a combination of complete relaxation and complete control. The body is awake, yet asleep. The same applies to the mind. The eyes may be closed and the mind seems asleep, yet the person is as alert as when wide awake.

Special forms of deep and regular breathing are part of the training. The purpose is to allow the body to reach a state much like the one that occurs before dropping off to sleep. Then tensions are gone,

In lotus position of Yoga, spine is erect while body and
mind relax through deep breathing. Diagram represents
centers of spiritual and physical energy along spine and
the opened mind as a thousand-petaled lotus.

Sanskrit word *OM*,
the sound of peace,
used as a blessing
and in Yoga chants.

there is a sense of peace, the mind is quiet, and the person becomes aware of a sense of unity with life. The most advanced practitioners can gain intuitive understanding quite beyond the ordinary.

Yoga teaches that the body has a series of centers, which are both physical and spiritual, located along the spine from its base up to the head. When one becomes aware of these control centers, one feels energy working through them. The entire spine seems to be charged electrically like a magnet stimulated by larger currents. Indeed, modern science has discovered that the body is basically electrical, and, of course, the spinal column carries both the conscious nervous system and the automatic nervous system controlling the heartbeat, breathing, and other activities. Scientists have discovered that during the state of meditation the brain may produce electrical patterns called *alpha* and *theta* waves. These patterns can stimulate creative thinking and improve awareness. Thus, Yoga's ability to bring a sense of health and well being to body and mind is not surprising.

Another important religion developed in northern India, near Benares, about 560 B.C. There a prince was born and given the name Siddhartha Gautama. According to legends a wise man predicted at the time of his birth that he would become an influential political or religious leader. Gautama's father was determined that the boy should inherit his title of rajah, so he trained him to the life of a ruler. He confined his son within the palace walls and kept him from any outside distractions. In time, Siddhartha Gautama married and had a son of his own.

Despite the pleasant surroundings, Gautama was not content. One day, the story is told, he had four experiences that changed his life. He happened to venture outside the walls and for the first time saw an old man so crippled by the infirmities of age that he was barely able to stand. Next Gautama came upon a person with a fatal disease lying beside the road. Then he observed a corpse. Lastly he noticed a beggar, holding up his bowl and asking for alms. These four encounters led Gautama to understand that there was great sorrow and suffering in the world.

When he was twenty-nine years old, Gautama made a decision that was to shake the world. One night he left his family, traded his princely garments for the common clothes of a servant, and journeyed off to search for a new life. He soon met two Hindu yogis, or teachers, and became their disciple, studying the causes of suffering. Before long Gautama decided that he had learned all the yogis could teach him, and he joined a band of men who believed that the needs of the body were the cause of evil. With them, he practiced fasting until he could subsist on as little as one bean a day. In time, he achieved his goal and his stomach touched his spine, but he still was not satisfied with his life.

Finally he studied mystic concentration and the control of the mind. He practiced these disciplines until all became still within him. One day he sat down under a fig tree and vowed not to leave the spot until he had gained complete understanding of the causes of suffering. His mind was tempted by every sort of distraction, but he resisted. Suddenly, like the bursting of a bubble, his very being broke from its shell, and he became enlightened. For many days he was lost in bliss.

When he arose, he set out to teach men the understanding that had come to him. Although the story of his life has become a mixture of fact and legend, it probably is an accurate reflection of Gautama's intentions. For almost fifty years he roamed the countryside, speaking to those who would listen. He founded an order of monks, spoke against the confused religious practices of the time, and offered simple and practical steps to enlightenment. His philosophy had no fixed beliefs, and he urged people to discover the truth of life through their personal experiences. He came to be called the Buddha, *the enlightened one.*

The religion of the Buddha ignored many current beliefs. He taught that one should not accept religious traditions from another, including himself. He taught men to question all authority over their

life. He taught no rituals. He refused to argue such
questions as the existence of God or the beginning
of the world. He taught people to avoid all forms
of superstition and worship of the supernatural.
What he said, in short, was: Look to nothing ex-
ternal. Light the lamp within yourself and work
out your own path with diligence.

The Buddha taught that the natural condition of
life on earth is that of suffering. Birth, sickness, old
age, death come to all. The suffering caused by
these events is due only to an unnatural view of life.
Fear and selfishness are what create suffering, and
the solution is to overcome personal desire. In fact,
the Buddha was preaching the original Hindu virtue
of detachment in an extremely simple way.

The Buddha offered eight basic steps a person
could take to achieve release and enlightenment.
They are as follows:

RIGHT KNOWLEDGE. The realization that the path to
enlightenment can be understood by all.

RIGHT MOTIVES. Whatever we want we eventually will
get. All choices must move us to the goal of truth.

RIGHT SPEECH. We must control our words so that they

Above: Buddhist eight-spoke "wheel of the law," representing the eightfold path to right living. *Below*: Lotus with eight central petals represents both new life and the eightfold path.

Right: Bronze statue, symbol of the Buddha with hands in gesture of peace.

are charitable and truthful, eliminating all that are not
of this nature.

RIGHT BEHAVIOR. All of our actions should reflect lack
of selfishness. All things should be done in love.

RIGHT OCCUPATION. Whatever life work one chooses
must be free of distractions from the goal of truth and
must not cause harm to others.

RIGHT EFFORT. Man must control his will so that his
acts will be in the right direction at the right time.
Thus, no efforts are withheld and none are wasted.

RIGHT MINDFULNESS. The best man will be aware of
himself, his own weaknesses and potentials. He will
examine himself and teach himself.

RIGHT MEDITATION. When the mind is empty of all
desires and all limitations, it is free to receive the
eternal.

Many separate sects have developed within Buddhism. Since the Buddha did not formulate rituals
or theology, men of very differing views can belong
to this religion. One example is the discipline called
Zen. A practice that evolved out of Buddhism, it
was developed by a monk named Bodhidharma
about a thousand years after the Buddha lived.
Around 500 A.D. Bodhidharma came to China
from India and taught there. Later his beliefs

spread to Japan and have been handed down through the generations by the monks who came after him. Today Zen is of much interest to the Western world as well.

Zen is as simple as it is hard to understand. It is similar to yoga in that a sitting position is used to achieve body control and encourage meditation. One method of teaching Zen is through koans, or riddles, which have no logical answers. The belief is that the mind itself is a barrier to mental freedom. When one is certain that logic will solve a problem, he may block greater understanding and true experience. Hence, the Zen teacher sets out to change that certainty again and again. The pupil is forced to abandon his belief in logical thinking and, in sudden flashes, gains true wisdom that cannot be described with any words.

Here are some typical Zen koans told by a Zen master to his students:

Late one night a blind man was about to go home after visiting a friend. He said to his friend, "Please, may I take your lantern with me?"

"Why carry a lantern?" asked the friend. "You cannot see any better with it."

"Perhaps not," said the blind man, "but others may see me and not bump into me."

So his friend gave the blind man the lantern of bamboo strips with a candle inside. The blind man, carrying the lantern, had gone only a short distance when someone bumped into him with great force. The blind man shouted out in anger, "Look out, why don't you see this lantern?"

"Why don't you light the candle?" asked the other.

Once a young, brash student named Yamakota visited the master, Dokuon. Wanting to impress the master, he said, "There is no mind, there is no body, there is no Buddha. There is no better, there is no worse. There is no master, and there is no student. There is no giving and no receiving. What we think we see and feel is not real. All that is real is emptiness. None of these things really exists."

Dokuon had been sitting quietly smoking his pipe. Suddenly he picked up his staff and gave Yamakota a terrible whack. The young student jumped up and cried out in anger.

"Since none of these things really exists and all is emptiness," said Dokuon, "where does your anger come from?"

Many consider that Buddhism strengthens the basic concepts of Hinduism. However, one of the chief differences between the two religions is that

Buddhists reject the caste system. Today Hinduism can be found in India, Pakistan, Ceylon, and Burma. Buddhism is scattered through parts of China, Japan, Ceylon, Burma, Thailand, Korea, Vietnam, and Tibet. Both religions have been adopted by peoples who have other faiths in addition. For centuries the ideas of Hinduism and Buddhism have been a powerful force in Asia and in parts of the Western world as well.

Taoism,
Confucianism,
and Shinto

Between 500 and 600 B.C. there lived two men who undoubtedly influenced Chinese life more than any other religious thinkers before or since. One was named Lao-tzu, the other K'ung Fu Tzu, or, as we say, Confucius. Lao-tzu was probably born around 600 B.C., and Confucius perhaps fifty years later. The two are said to have met, and Confucius had great respect for the older man. In fact, Confucius is supposed to have given him the name of Lao-tzu, which means *old philosopher.*

However, the teachings of the two men are in many ways quite the opposite of each other. Still, each is valuable, and together they complement one another.

An early Chinese historian tells us that Lao-tzu was a curator of one of the royal libraries of the Chou dynasty. His countrymen were badly oppressed, and life's basic values seemed all but lost. Deeply disturbed by the unhappiness around him, Lao-tzu decided to leave his job, and he began traveling alone toward the West. Eventually he reached the pass leading from China to the lands beyond, where he was recognized by a warden of the frontier whose name was Kwan Yin. Like Lao-tzu, Kwan Yin was a philosopher familiar with many of the fine and noble principles cherished by past generations.

Kwan Yin urged that Lao-tzu write down his views and teachings for others to follow. Lao-tzu agreed and left his book, divided into two parts, in the safekeeping of the warden before going on his way. He was not seen again.

Lao-tzu's writings have been of great influence.

His book is short, and the statements in it are written in simple, poetic fashion. Some of the sayings probably existed long before the master gathered them together, but all show the stamp of his personality.

His book is called the *Tao-Te Ching,* and his beliefs are called Taoism. Tao is a Chinese word, meaning *way,* or *path.* In it Lao-tzu writes in part:

> The Tao that can be walked upon is not the unchanging path. The name that can be named is not the enduring name.

> The highest excellence is like water. The virtue of water is in its benefit to all things, and in its effortless filling of the low places that are disliked by men. Its way is like that of the Tao.

Chinese symbol for water, the life giver.

Taoist symbol
for yang and yin,
the opposites that
work together.

The Tao is hidden and has no name. But the Tao is able to give to all things that which they need and which makes them complete.

With all the sharpness of the Way of Heaven, it injures not. With all the doing in the way of the wise man, he does not strive.

To Lao-tzu, a person could understand this hidden way, or hidden force, only by accepting it and moving with it. He taught that the Tao worked in sets of opposites, the opposites becoming the whole. The Chinese symbol of the circle containing two interlocking shapes that move around each other expresses the idea vividly. The two halves of the circle, one dark and one light, are called "yang and

yin." Each is the opposite of the other, and they sym-
bolize the concept of opposites working together,
such as the principles of male and female and the
balance of positive and negative forces in the universe. One must look always for that opposite which
is the most obscure.

> The seeing of what is small is the secret of clear sight.
> The guarding of what is soft is the secret of strength.

> The movement of the Tao proceeds by contraries.
> Weakness marks the course of Tao's accomplishments.

Taoism also states the principle of the trinity,
which is found in many religions.

> The Tao produced one.
> One produced two.
> Two produced three.
> Three produced all things.

Ancient Chinese symbol
of infinite trinity.

Many Taoist writings have appeared since the time of Lao-tzu, but none are more basically and simply expressed.

Confucius was born into a family of the common people in the Province of Lu. Although he became a teacher of some of the more well-to-do of his day, his ambition was to hold a prominent state office. In that position his teachings would have wider influence. Finally he became a law officer in the ministry of justice. Not content with this lowly position, he left the post and traveled from state to state looking for a ruler who would understand and support his religious ideas.

Confucius was convinced that the great Chinese rulers before his time had governed justly and that his people once had understood the way a good life should be lived. Thus, he believed that tradition held the answer to the many social and political problems of the day. If the country would follow again the rules of conduct passed down by the ancestors, then conditions would be set to rights.

Instead of addressing himself to philosophical arguments, Confucius concentrated on the relation-

ships between members of a family and members
of society. Where Lao-tzu's teachings were poetic
and abstract, those of Confucius had to do with
practical matters of everyday life. He taught cour-
tesy and good manners. He taught that if such
practices began in the family, they would spread
through the community and eventually help to solve
the problems of state government.

To illustrate his points, Confucius used short
saying or proverbs that had come down through
the centuries. Although he may have originated
some of them, he thought of himself as a teacher
who was passing on the best knowledge of the past.
After his death, the sayings were compiled in a book
called Lun Yu, which means *analects,* or *collected
sayings.*

Many of the sayings stress moderation: the good
path is usually that which avoids extremes and con-
siders all viewpoints equally before moving ahead.
The following quotes from the Lun Yu are examples
of some of Confucius's principles:

> Those who behave well toward their parents and older
> brothers seldom fight the authority of their superiors.

It is upon that which is basic that a good man works.
Then the Way grows. Surely proper behavior toward
parents and elder brothers is the way of goodness?

Clever talk and a pretentious manner are seldom found
in the good man.

He who rules by moral force is like the polestar, which
remains in its place while all the lesser stars do homage
to it.

He who by reanimating the old can gain knowledge
of the new is fit to be a teacher.

The good man does not preach what he practices until
he has practiced what he preaches.

A good man can see a question from all sides without
bias. The small man can see a question from one side
only.

The good man does not grieve that other people do
not recognize his merits. His only worry is that he
should fail to recognize theirs.

While other religions have spread from country
to country, the religion called Shinto began in Japan
and has remained there. Although Shinto is Japa-

nese, the name was borrowed from the Chinese words *shen,* meaning *good spirits,* and *tao,* meaning *the way.* So Shen-tao, or Shinto, means *the way of the good spirits.*

The story of Shinto begins with a legend. It says that after the creator Kami formed the world, there were many spirits and lesser gods. Two of them were Izanagi and Izanami. One day they looked down from the bridge of heaven and wondered what was below. Deciding to investigate, Izanagi took a jeweled spear and lowered the point. As he moved it around it splashed into the ocean below. When he raised the spear, the salt water on it dried into large, pearly drops, which fell back into the ocean and formed the islands of Japan. "Let us go down and live on those islands," decided the two gods. So they descended and subsequently gave birth to three noble children: the sun goddess and her brothers, the moon god and the storm god. The sun goddess had children, and, according to legend, her grandson became the first emperor of Japan.

For centuries Japan followed the religion of the

rising sun, and the emperor was believed by many to be divine. Shinto remained the state religion until Japan was defeated in the Second World War. Then Emperor Hirohito denied publicly that he was of divine descent. However, Shinto has survived this disavowal, and belief in Kami is still strong in Japan today.

Part II
RELIGIONS
OF THE
WEST

Parsiism

Many of the ideas that are part of the Judaism and Christianity which spread westward came from a religion whose followers are known as Parsis. It was founded by a man named Zarathustra, who is more frequently referred to by his Greek name, Zoroaster. The name Parsi comes from the Indian word for Persia, which is where the religion began. It went from there to India and still is practiced in the area around Bombay today.

Zoroaster may have lived around 600 B.C. His

origins are obscure, and there is some evidence that there were a series of men who all were given the name Zoroaster. The account here may refer only to one of the people to bear his name.

Supposedly Zoroaster was born the son of a camel merchant. At that time life was very hard. The people worshiped many gods, and the priests were in conflict. Frequently the country was engaged in savage warfare, fighting off invaders. Zoroaster received a fine education, studying under some of the best teachers in Persia. Later he worked on the battlefields, helping to care for the wounded, and traveled many places in order to minister to his starving and suffering countrymen.

Often he went alone to a high mountain, Sabalan, to meditate upon life's problems. At the age of thirty he experienced visions, which revealed to him the nature of life and truth. Thereafter, he devoted himself to bringing his revelations to people in all walks of life. One account tells of his encounter with a prince who doubted the validity of his teaching and threw him into prison. Meanwhile, the prince's favorite horse became incurably lame; all the physicians, wise men, and magicians in the royal court could not heal it. Finally Zoroaster was given permission to go to the ailing horse, and he was able to cure it completely. Thereafter, the prince became one of Zoroaster's supporters. This story may refer to Prince Vistaspa, who controlled part of eastern Iran and supported Zoroaster's claim to be a prophet.

Legend tells that Zoroaster had great difficulty in getting the people to understand his message. Later, during one of his country's battles, an enemy broke into the temple and stabbed him when at prayer fatally in the back.

One precept revealed to Zoroaster through his visions was the existence of a single creator, whom Zoroaster called Ahura Mazda. Ahura means *lord,* and Mazda means *light,* and so the full name translates as *god of eternal light.* Zoroaster said the Ahura Mazda sent forth a holy guiding spirit, representing all that was good, and also a twin spirit, representing all that was evil. Later the holy spirit of good often was spoken of as Ahura Mazda himself, and the evil spirit was considered his opponent. Thus, the concept of the duality of good and evil became the basis of Zoroaster's religion.

The Zoroastrian sacred book, called the Avesta, is said to have been dictated by Zoroaster to Prince Vistaspa and recorded on calf skins. Several times invaders destroyed parts of the sacred record, but most of it has been preserved through the centuries.

The Avesta states that the god of light carries out his activities through six forces. In this way the older beliefs in many gods and goddesses were harmonized with Zoroaster's idea of unity. In fact, the names of the six forces were borrowed from some of those gods worshiped earlier by the Indians and the Persians. According to Zoroaster, these

Sun symbol for
Ahura-Mazda,
God of eternal
light and wisdom.

chosen six are not gods but characteristics or extensions of the one god, Ahura Mazda.

In the Avesta the names are given as follows:

Ahura Mazda, god of eternal light

Asha, right and justice

Vohu Manah, good mind

Khshathra, power and dominion

Armaiti, reverence

Haurvatat, perfection

Ameretati, immortality

The idea of the sacred seven was not new, for many of the ancient religions symbolized god as a seven-headed serpent with a central head flanked by three on each side. Early Indian drawings and figures often depict a person with one head, four arms, and two legs. The extensions represent the sacred seven in humanized form.

There are many parallels between the Christian and Jewish Bible and the Avesta. The Avesta states that the world was created in six days and tells the story of the first man and woman who were placed in a garden called Paradise. Like Adam and Eve,

Shiva, Hindu god of dance, also represents the sacred seven in human form as the central head and six limbs of movement.

they were forced to leave because they disobeyed their god. Many ancient religions describe such a paradise, those in Asia often locating it in the East, while some in the Americas locate it in the West. One suggestion is that this paradise, or garden of Eden, might refer to a destroyed civilization situated in the Pacific Ocean. At any rate, the story appears in similar form all over the world.

Zoroaster also proclaimed a golden rule much like the one presented later in the Christian New Testament. It, too, states that no one should do to another that which he would not wish to have done to himself. The Avesta taught the existence of both a heaven and a hell and the judgment of the soul at the time of death. It says, "The dead shall rise, life shall return to their bodies, and they shall breathe again." Zoroaster also is quoted as saying that those who believed in him "would not perish, but be given eternal life."

Some of Zoroaster's teachings are expressed in these hymns which have been translated from the Avesta itself:

In the beginning the twin spirits declared their nature,
The good and the evil, in thought, word, and deed.
Between the two the wise ones choose well;
Not so the foolish.

As the holy one I recognized you, O Wise Lord,
When at the beginning of existence I saw you
Appoint justice for deed and word;
Evil reward to the evil, good to the good,
Through your wisdom at the last turning point of
    creation.

These things are clear to the man of insight:
He who through good mind knows righteousness as
   the ruler,
He serves these ideals in word and deed.
He shall be, O Wise Lord, your devoted guest.

The best possession of Zoroaster has been revealed.
It is that the Wise Lord has granted, through the right,
Eternal bliss to him and to all others who have known
   and practiced
The words and deeds of his good religion.

Today the Parsis preserve their religion with a number of simple rituals. In the central room of each temple is an ever-burning fire of sandalwood, symbolizing the eternal light of Ahura Mazda. If the fire should go out in one temple, it is relit with burning coals carried from another temple. In an outer court of each temple is kept a white bull, which is a symbol of God's creative power in the world of living things. The Parsis do not worship the fire or the bull, but believe they are symbols much like the baptismal bowl or altar of Christianity.

The most unusual custom of present-day practice is the ritual for those who have died. Bodies are placed on ledges above the roof of the temple, where vultures and other birds pick the bones clean. Parsis feel that in this way the material substance of the body is returned naturally as a gift to the living.

Today, although there are perhaps only 140,000 members of the Parsi religion, the influence of the faith is felt throughout the world.

Judaism

The story of the Jewish religion begins perhaps 4000 years ago. According to legend, a man called Abraham was born in the area known today as Iraq. The members of Abraham's tribe of desert dwellers worshiped many idols. One day Abraham took an axe and smashed all those in his home. At first his father was very angry, but Abraham convinced him that the idols were worthless. He said that instead one ought to believe in the active and lasting forces in nature. However, many in the tribe would not accept these ideas, so Abraham and some of his relatives left and went west across the rivers Tigris and Euphrates. They became called Ibris, or Hebrews, which in one translation means *those who came across.*

The tribe of Abraham increased, becoming strong and self-sufficient. However, a famine came to the land. It caused great hardship, and the tribe was forced to move into Egypt, where food was more plentiful. They settled in Goshen near the Nile River and prospered there. Still, they kept their religious ideas distinct from those of the Egyptians. This refusal of the Hebrews to accept the popular religion worried the Egyptians. They felt threatened by the strange teachings. Finally the Egyptians forced the Hebrews into slavery, believing that they then would have to adopt Egyptian ways.

The accounts say that the Egyptians still were not satisfied. Accordingly, the Egyptian king passed a law commanding that all the male Hebrew babies must be drowned. Thus, the Hebrew girls could only marry Egyptians, and their children would be brought up as Egyptians.

Among the endangered Hebrew boys was one

who, according to some accounts, had been born to an Egyptian father and a Hebrew mother. The mother lived in the Hebrew community, and so she feared greatly for the baby's life. To hide his identity, the mother placed the baby in a basket of reeds and set it afloat on the Nile River. By chance, the king's daughter happened to be near the river and found the basket. She brought the healthy baby boy home with her to the king's court and there cared for him. He was named Moses after part of the king's name, Ramoses.

Whatever the details of his life, Moses became a man of two worlds. Exposed to the best teachings of Egyptian religion and tradition, he also had much sympathy for the Hebrews. One day Moses saw some Hebrew slaves being beaten by an Egyptian. Without hesitation, Moses attacked the Egyptian and killed him. The incident created more hostility between the Hebrews and Egyptians, and Moses became a hunted man.

Several stories are told of how Moses persuaded the Egyptian king to let him and his people leave Egypt to find a new place to live. According to the most familiar one, Egypt became afflicted with plagues of insects and disease, which the king felt were warnings from the gods.

After being granted their freedom, the Hebrews wandered across the desert for many years, finally reaching the base of Mount Sinai. The long journey became known as the Exodus. There Moses went alone to the mountaintop to meditate on the plight of his people. When he returned, many days later, he brought a clear message. Moses said that one god, Yahweh, had appeared to him and revealed the commands that the Hebrews must follow. According to tradition, the first five books of the Jewish Bible were written by Moses and contain the laws that he received while on the mountain. In the second book of the Jewish Bible, Exodus, which tells the story of the flight from Egypt, a group of these commands are listed. Ten of them are considered the basis of Jewish belief and conduct, and most of them can be found in the codes of other ancient religions. They are:

There is no other God than Yahweh.
Worship no idol or image of any kind.
Do not take the name of Yahweh in vain.

Rest every seventh day on the day that is holy.

Honor your father and motner.

Do not commit murder.

Do not commit adultery.

Do not steal.

Do not give false testimony.

Do not covet the possessions of others.

In addition, the first group of books of the Jewish Bible includes hundreds of laws and regulations that were said to have come from God through Moses. While some of them are quite practical, others seem strange to us today. Certain rules listed the animals or birds that could or could not be eaten. Some foods were forbidden for reasons of public health.

For the Jews, the Ten Commandments meant that God had chosen them for special responsibilities. They felt that God had entered their lives to change the course of history; theirs was a special destiny. After the death of Moses, the Jews became a strong nation, winning many battles and expanding their territory. Indeed, the nation was called Israel from a name meaning, *God fights*. The nation reached the height of its power in the era of the

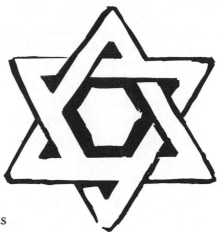

Jewish Star of David,
matching triangles of
the ancients, symbolizing
physical and spiritual worlds
inverted but interlocked.

great kings: Saul, David, and Solomon. The city
of Jerusalem became the stronghold of the Jews, and
the nation became secure for a time.

Much of the Jewish Bible is the history of this
nation. Parts of it read like an enormous family tree
while other sections contain psalms, or hymns, some
of which are attributed to King David. The best
of them have found their way into religious songs
that are still sung today, and the words are familiar
to many people.

> The Lord is my shepherd; I shall not want.
> He makes me to lie down in green pastures;
> He leads me beside the still waters.

He restores my soul; He leads me in the paths
  of righteousness for His name's sake.

Make a joyful noise unto the Lord, all the lands.
Serve the Lord with gladness;
Come before his presence with singing.

The Book of Proverbs, which contains hundreds of wise sayings, is another well-known section. It is like a chapter of the wisdom of Confucius tucked into the middle of Jewish history. Here are several of the proverbs said to have been spoken by the wise king, Solomon:

The man who boasts of a false ability is like wind and clouds without rain.

A proper word, well-spoken, is like apples of gold in pictures of silver.

He who has no rule over his own spirit is like a broken-down city without walls.

Take the impurities from the silver, and the cup which is made is fit for the finest.

The religious history of the Jews covers a long sweep of time. It includes the words of numerous, influential prophets. According to tradition, one of them, named Ezra, transcribed the first books of the Jewish Bible, called the Pentateuch, after their destruction in the temple about 587 B.C. Throughout the message of the prophets appears the idea that a great religious leader, a messiah, would come in the future. Those who follow Judiasm believe that the messiah has not yet arrived; he is still awaited.

Judaism began as a tribal religion, but today is a worldwide faith. The Ten Commandments have become part of the social and ethical structure of

Menorah, symbol of light and the seven-day week of the Jewish faith.

much of the Western world. The work week in the West still follows the basic pattern of six days of activity and one of rest. The Western code of justice and its legal system reflects the religion that began in the time of Moses.

Today Judaism has over thirteen million members. Of these, more than half live in North and South America, most in the United States. Between three and four million are in the countries of Europe, mainly Russia and Poland, and about two million are in Asia, most of whom now live in the new Jewish State of Israel.

Israel lies on the eastern shore of the Mediterranean Sea. About 250 miles long and in places only 15 miles wide, its ownership has changed perhaps forty times. At present Israel includes part of the newer section of the historic city of Jerusalem. To those living there today, Judaism has returned to its homeland after centuries of wandering.

No people have been so scattered as the Jews, and they have suffered many persecutions as they have been forced to move over the world. Still, Jews have maintained great unity. In 1948, the Israeli prime minister, David Ben-Gurion, read the country's new Declaration of Independence, and the Israeli national anthem was played. This song, called "Hatikvoh," or "The Hope," perhaps best represents the continuing faith of the people of Abraham and Moses.

Christianity

Among the various groups that developed within first century Judaism, one became an important link between Judaism and Christianity. These people are known as the Essenes, and their existence has been the subject of much study in recent years.

In 1947, Arabs discovered numerous clay pots containing scrolls and writing in caves among the rocks surrounding the Dead Sea. These writings once were part of a library that existed before the time of Jesus, and they have come to be called the Dead Sea Scrolls. Among the fragments of parchment are the earliest existing copies of some of the first books in the Old Testament of the Christian Bible. In addition, they include many other biblical writings that were thought to be lost.

The library belonged to the Essenes, whose name means *expectancy*. They were a group of scholars and mystics who had preserved much of the teachings of the Jewish prophets, and they believed in the coming of the messiah as predicted by the prophets. The Essenes lived a communal life in which everyone, including women, were considered equals, and all possessions belonged to the community.

Among the manuscripts of the Essenes are several that show some of the links between Christianity and other earlier religions. One book is called, *The War of the Sons of Light with the Sons of Darkness*. It dramatizes the conflict between good and evil much as Zoraster expressed it. The Essenes felt that they, as God's elect, would be victorious while all enemies would perish in a final battle. Another manuscript is the book of Enoch, which is made up of the combined writings of several men over a period of time. In Enoch and other

Essene writings can be found many concepts that were later echoed in the Gospels of the Christian Bible.

Not much is known about the actual life of Jesus. According to the accounts in the Christian Bible, he was born in the stable of an inn at Bethlehem in Judea. Wise men who were astrologers arrived in the vicinity and told King Herod, Governor of Jerusalem, that they were following a bright star in the skies in order to find a baby destined to become a great king. Various accounts describe this bright star, which was visible at the time. Astronomers have calculated since then that several years before the date now used for Jesus' birth there was a conjunction, or lineup, of the planets Venus, Jupiter, and Saturn, along with one of the distant stars, and they would have appeared almost at the same spot in the sky. The combined light may have been the bright star described.

According to the Bible, King Herod immediately issued an order that all the baby boys of the Jews should be killed. Thus, Jesus' family was forced to flee to Egypt, where they remained until the death of Herod. Then they returned and settled in

Nazareth about fifty miles north of Jerusalem. While still a boy Jesus worked with his father as a carpenter.

Until some of the recent manuscript discoveries, many scholars felt that Jesus received a minimal education and did not travel much. However, various sources now suggest that this belief may not be so. Some scholars have claimed that both Jesus and John the Baptist may have been members of the Essene community for a time, or at least that Jesus was acquainted with the manuscripts, teachings, and customs of this group. Tibetan legends tell of Jesus studying in Tibet and becoming a great master. Whether such legends are true or not, Jesus certainly was exposed to a wide variety of Jewish and Near Eastern traditions.

According to the Christian Bible, Jesus used withdrawal and meditation as a way to open himself to religious understanding. Like Zoroaster, Jesus began traveling among his people as a teacher and a healer at the age of about thirty. His methods were startling. He spoke alike to rich men, priests, laborers, and criminals. His only occupation was to minister to the needs of others. He healed souls

as well as bodies and knew the background of
people he met for the first time without a word
being spoken. He taught by means of stories, or
parables, letting his listeners draw their own con-
clusions. He told people to give up their possessions,
much as the Essenes had done, and begin life over
again. He preached that people should do good to
their enemies even at the risk of death. Among
many of his statements are the following:

Love your neighbor as yourself.

You shall know the truth and the truth shall make
you free.

Come to me, all who are heavy-laden, and I will give
you rest.

Jesus did not follow accepted rules and regulations. The story is related in the Christian Bible
that he was eating at the house of some lawyers
on the Sabbath. While there, Jesus discovered that
a man was very ill and ministered to him. The
lawyers sat silently. Clearly they disapproved of
this work that Jesus was doing on the day of rest.
Jesus challenged them with the remark, "Which of
you, if you found your ox had fallen into a pit,

would not set to work and pull him out on the Sabbath?"

About the problems of state he said, "Give to Caesar those things which are Caesar's, but give to God your Father those things which belong to him."

In 63 B.C., Jerusalem had become a part of the Roman Empire. Rome governed the country through a Jewish king, but maintained many troops and government officials there. Although Jesus wielded no power, his presence and his message of nonviolence did not pass unnoticed by the Roman authorities. Later his entry into Jerusalem was made in the style of the early Jewish kings on the royal

Christian Chi-Rho, symbol combining first two letters of Greek word for Christ.

beast, the donkey. The Romans could not decide
what his purpose was and became concerned.

To those who could not grasp the significance
of Jesus' teachings, his enthusiastic band of followers became a threat. Eventually he was arrested
by the Romans and brought before Pontius Pilate,
procurator of Judea. Pilate could find no fault with
him and, refusing to take the responsibility for
judgment, turned him over to the mob, who wished
him destroyed. Jesus made no effort to appease
his enemies or to escape. Placing a crown of thorns
upon his head, the mob forced him to drag a heavy
wooden cross to the place of execution. There, according to the custom of the time, he was crucified.
The full impact of Jesus' ministry was not felt
until his death. According to the Christian Bible,
his tomb later was found empty. He appeared to
various of his disciples, bringing them the message
of his resurrection from the dead. The small band
of twelve or so men who had traveled with him
felt his living presence so strongly that they spread
word of his victory over death far and wide. The
event became the core of the Christian religion,

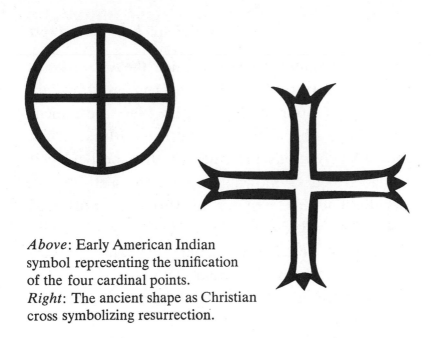

Above: Early American Indian symbol representing the unification of the four cardinal points.
Right: The ancient shape as Christian cross symbolizing resurrection.

which formed around the life of Jesus. Christianity taught a threefold message: the infinite mercy of God, the truth of universal love, and the victory of mankind over death.

The first section of the Christian Bible, which was taken from the Jewish Bible, is called the Old Testament. The second section is called the New Testament. It describes the birth of Christianity. Jesus wrote nothing down, and accounts of his life passed orally from one generation to another for

perhaps one hundred years. Then they were codi-
fied. The story of Jesus' life and teachings appears
in the first four books of the New Testament
ascribed to the Apostles Matthew, Mark, Luke
and John. Various activities of the apostles then
are described. Following are letters sent by the
Apostle Paul as sermons to various groups and
cities. They represent his personal insights into the
meaning of Jesus' life. Letters by James, Peter,
John, and Jude are recorded. The New Testament
ends with predictions made by John in a book called
Revelation.

The whole group of writings is surprisingly short.
Much of the content echoes the prophetic themes
preserved by the Essenes. The predicted messiah,
or Christ, has come. In the future there will be a
second coming. It will be the time of judgment
when all will be called on to account for themselves.
God's reward of eternal life awaits those who are
resurrected.

The New Testament writer named Paul started
his career as a Jew who actively assisted in the
Roman persecution of the early Christians. Later

he was converted to their beliefs and spread word of the new religion zealously. He traveled to Syria and Macedonia, to the Mediterranean islands of Crete and Sicily, and to Rome. Wherever he went he made converts. While in Rome he was arrested by Emperor Nero, but after his release continued to preach there. By the time of Paul's death Christianity had established strong roots in many areas of the Roman Empire.

To many people the single Christian God of love, mercy, and eternal life was a simple and fulfilling concept. As Christianity gained followers, members of the new faith were persecuted relentlessly. Finally, in the year 312 A.D., the Emperor Constantine became a convert and declared Christianity the state religion of the Roman Empire.

The seat of the Empire was then at Constantinople, but church leaders in Rome thought of themselves as the leaders of the new faith. Thus, the Latin-speaking Christians of Rome broke away from the Greek-speaking Christians of the East and founded the Roman Catholic Church. The other branch became the Eastern Orthodox Church.

The word *catholic* means *universal,* and indeed

the aim of the Church of Rome was to make Christianity the universal state religion of the vast Roman Empire. Roman Catholicism spread rapidly through the growing nations of Europe. The church leaders, called popes, who were selected in Rome, gained great power in both the religious and political life of the people of Europe.

Probably no religion has spread as fast or brought more hope than Christianity. At the same time no religion has caused more suffering. Historians consider Christianity partly responsible for the time in Europe called the Dark Ages, which occurred about the twelfth and thirteenth centuries. Scientific thought was at a low ebb. People believed the earth was flat and that the sun went around the earth. They became interested in magic and superstition. The Roman Church prevented the people from reading books that spoke against the doctrines of the Church. Those who found fault with the Church were punished, much as the early Romans had persecuted the first Christians. In the thirteenth century came the Inquisition. People who refused to accept the Christianity of the Roman Church were tortured and put to death.

During these same centuries, the Christians organized holy wars, called "crusades," in the name of the Church. Armies marched long distances to fight the unbelievers of the Near East, whose strength was thought to threaten the power of Christianity. The era was an unhappy time in the history of Europe and the growth of Christianity.

After the Dark Ages Europe emerged into the period of scientific and artistic development

Left: High-reaching Gothic cathedrals raised the crossbar of the Christian cross toward heaven. *Below*: Contemporary Christian symbol of worship using the shape of the cross.

known as the Renaissance. The old philosophies of the Greeks and Romans stimulated new thought, and religious reformers came forward to speak out against the injustices of the Church.

In England, John Wycliffe translated the Old and New Testaments from Latin into English. The German monk, Martin Luther, nailed his now famous list of complaints against the Church on the door of the castle church in Wittenberg. He objected to the practice of selling indulgences, which people bought so that their sins would be forgiven, in order to raise money for the building of cathedrals in Rome. Luther wrote many books outlining his beliefs. He felt that "no man can command or ought to command, or by force compel any man's belief." Luther went on to translate the Old and New Testaments into German.

These people and many others who protested against the existing rules of the Church became called protestants. Other leaders of this movement appeared: Ulrich Zwingli in Switzerland, John Calvin in France and later Switzerland, and John Knox in Scotland. At about the same time, the Church of England separated from the Roman Church, keeping many of the traditions of worship, but demanding freedom from any outside authority.

The Christian Church has continued to break up into a vast number of groups. Some of them are very similar; others hold almost opposing views. Many sects were transplanted to the New World after the time of Columbus. Some, such as that of the Mormons, sprang up later in the United States itself. Today almost one out of every three persons is some kind of Christian. Certain groups believe Jesus Christ is God, while others see him as a great humanitarian. Some concentrate on specific rituals and statements of belief, while others, such as the Society of Friends have no prescribed beliefs and no ministers. Christianity is a vast network that has grown out of the ideas of God, mercy, love, truth, and eternal life taught by the carpenter named Jesus almost 2000 years ago.

Islam

As Christianity was spreading, another influential religious leader appeared. Around the year 570 A.D., a young Arab was born to a family named Hashem, probably in the city of Mecca. Some accounts say his father died before he was born, but others claim that his parents died when he was young. At any rate, the boy, named Muhammad, grew up first with his grandfather and then with one of his uncles. He became a camel driver, accompanying many caravans on long trips. His travels took him to areas where he met both Jews and Christians, and so he learned something about their religions and traditions. Muhammad could not read, but he heard certain stories from the religious books of both Christians and Jews. He was impressed with the Jewish prophets, who had unified their people into a nation.

When Muhammad was twenty-five years old, he settled in Mecca as a merchant and married a wealthy woman named Khadija, much older than himself, to whom he was devoted. Although Muhammad was content with his life, he was upset by the conditions that existed around him. At that time the religion of the Arabs was in a disorganized state. There were temples, there was a god named Allah, and there were also local tribal gods associated with special places or sacred objects, such as stones. The early Hebrews, too, used a stone for their altar. Most Arabs paid only token attention to the gods, and there was much thievery and stealing. Caravans transporting goods from one place to another were robbed regularly by groups of desert dwellers.

Muhammad developed the practice of retreating

Star with good-luck crescent,
Muslim symbol of Islam.

to a cave to think things through by himself. He longed to be of some use to his people. According to tradition, during one of these sessions he suddenly was startled by a voice, although no one else was present. The voice was that of the Angel Gabriel, who commanded him to receive a message of hope for the Arabs. The angel showed Muhammad words that he was to carry to the people. Although Muhammad could not read, he found himself able to understand the words. In this way, say the Muslims, Muhammad received the sacred Koran. The Koran itself says nothing about a cave, however. The prophet describes his experience by saying that he saw a vision of a heavenly messenger during the day on the horizon.

At first Muhammad brought the message of the

Koran to his wife, telling her of the visions he had seen. Soon he convinced his relatives of the truth of his experience. Nevertheless, others were not ready to accept the words of the brash merchant turned prophet at the age of forty. Muhammad found converts in the slaves of the city of Mecca, but the merchants were irritated by this bold and self-proclaimed prophet. After ten years in Mecca, there was much opposition to him.

At this time Muhammad was invited to help settle a clan feud in the city of Medina. He hoped that the many Jews living there would accept his claim to be the true prophet following Moses and Jesus. The Jews in Medina also rejected him, however, as many Arabs in Mecca had done. Still, he finally gained the support he wanted. A small number of Muhammad's followers moved to Medina, and the people in Mecca became so hostile that Muhammad was forced to flee to Medina too.

In Medina, Muhammad built a temple, but he was not able to teach there peacefully. A group accused Muhammad of sending out a force to ambush some of his Arab enemies in Mecca. Fighting broke out, and a band of Muhammad's followers from Medina did organize an attack on a caravan of merchants from Mecca. The Meccans defended the caravan with an army and attacked Muhammad's group. Eventually two large armies met south

Muslim mosque with lofty minarets. From balcony the faithful are led in prayer.

of Medina, and Muhammad was victorious. This victory assured Muhammad's success as a leader. Later, eight years after he left Mecca, Muhammad and his armed followers returned to the city that had rejected him, and Mecca became the holy center of a new faith. It was called Islam, meaning *submission to God's will.*

Within a few years Islam developed into a powerful religion in the Arab lands. Even when Muhammad died, it continued to grow, for Muhammad had written in the Koran that he was only God's messenger to the people. Allah himself was eternal.

To Muslims, the Koran contains the words of the God, Allah. Nothing in the Koran ever has been changed, for Muslims believe each word to be sacred. The book is a group of short poetic sermons, later arranged so that the shortest ones are near the beginning and the longer ones near the end. The Koran relates the early history of the Arabs, and many of its stories parallel those in the Old Testament.

In both cases one can find the story of the two wives of Abraham, one named Sarah and the other named Hagar. Sarah was a Jew, and Hagar was an Arab. Each had children. Sarah became jealous of Hagar and forced Abraham to drive Hagar and her child into the desert. The offspring of Abraham and Hagar were the forefathers of the Arabs. In fact, the early Jews and Arabs intermarried and lived together closely in many places. Thus, some of the early religious practices developed by the Jews became a part of Arab belief too.

In the Koran are the stories of Noah and the flood, Moses and the Egyptians, and the lives of King David and King Solomon. There is also a section describing the birth of Jesus and honoring him as a true prophet of the one God, Allah. The Koran teaches that a great prophet will return in the future, much as the Jews predicted a messiah and the Christians predicted a second coming of Christ.

Many of the words of the Koran are hymns of praise to Allah or warnings against doing evil. The chapter "Daylight" says:

> By the light of day and by the fall of night, Your Lord has not forsaken you, nor does he hate you. The life to come holds a richer prize for you than this present life. You shall be grateful for what your Lord will

give you. Did he not find you an orphan and give you shelter? Did he not find you in error and guide you? Did he not find you poor and enrich you? Therefore do not wrong the orphan, nor send away the beggar. But proclaim the goodness of your Lord.

The chapter called "Night" relates:

For him that gives in charity and guards against evil and believes in goodness, We shall smooth the path of salvation; but for him that neither gives nor takes and does not believe in goodness, We shall afflict his path. When he breathes his last his riches will not help him.

Like the Bible, the Koran refers to the rewards of heaven and the punishments of hell. It proclaims the glory of the one God, Allah, and that Muhammad is his prophet, directed to teach and lead his people. Through the Koran, Muhammad outlined what became a system of beliefs and practices for his followers. It included six Articles of Belief, which were:

God is one; this one is Allah and Muhammad is his prophet.
The Koran is Allah's inspired book. It is the last in a

group of three, the law of Moses, the Gospel of Jesus, and the Koran of Muhammad.

The angels are God's messengers and aids, and there are evil spirits who oppose them.

God sent his prophets to earth in special times and places. The earlier prophets were Moses and Jesus. The last great prophet was Muhammad.

The Day of Judgment will balance evil against the good, and souls will pass to heaven or hell.

Although men are free to choose, their lives are planned by Allah who is all-knowing.

Clearly coupled with the Articles of Belief were the rituals called the Pillars of Faith, to be followed by all believers. They were:

Recite the creed of Islam at least once in a lifetime.

Pray five times each day.

Donate your tithe to the Church for the faith and for the poor.

Observe the fast in the holy month of Ramadan.

Visit the holy city of Mecca at least once in your lifetime.

During the next few centuries after Muhammad the Arabs, united in the new faith, became a large and expanding nation. Carried by wars of conquest, the religion of Islam spread in a long curve around the eastern shores of the Mediterranean Sea and westward across the north of Africa. The Arabs conquered the holy city of Jerusalem, and the Arabs known as Moors moved up into Spain, bringing the religion of Islam wherever they went. Money from the conquests poured into the Muslim empire. Great centers of learning sprang up, and the study of art and science flourished. At the time that Europe and Christianity were moving into the Dark Ages the Muslim lands were experiencing a renaissance that was only later to come to the nations of Europe.

Crusading armies sent by the Christians during the Holy Wars were defeated again and again by the Muslims. Finally battles in France pushed the Arabs back into Spain, and the two great religions existed in a sort of grand balance for a time. At last, however, Spain regained its freedom from the conquerors. The original aim of Muhammad to unite Arabs, Jews, and Christians in the spirit of a new religion had led to some of the bloodiest battles in history.

Later the Muslim empire broke up into independent states, but their religion of Islam remains strong. As late as 1947, a new Islamic state called Pakistan was carved out of two areas of northern India as a haven for Muslims when India gained independence from Britain.

Today many differences have been resolved, but conflicts still exist. What was in many ways a common religious heritage has had to survive a vast three-way split. Through the United Nations and the efforts of many individuals, a unification of ideals and purposes is being developed once again. It is a unification born of a past in which all three religions have made mistakes, yet all have similar goals.

The Muslim faith still grows in modern times. Perhaps one out of every seven people in the world honors the Koran and the Islam proclaimed by Muhammad, submission to God's will.

Part III
NEW TRENDS
IN FAITH

Science and
Religion

The reappearance of scientific thought in the West upset many beliefs about the world taught by the religious books. People began to question the old stories of gods coming to earth in human form, the story of creation, and accounts of miracles. Many felt that though they might be meaningful, they were not true in a factual sense. Charles R. Darwin, a nineteenth century English naturalist, introduced a theory of evolution that was especially influential. It suggested that life on earth had developed in a slow, step-by-step way and explained creation differently. Man was said to have evolved from an apelike being in the distant past.

But today science is exploring new areas. One of them is the consciousness of man. Laboratories are studying evidence that consciousness can function apart from a physical body. Groups like the Psychical Research Foundation in North Carolina are examining scientific evidence of life after death. Psychiatrists, such as Doctor Ian Stevenson, are investigating cases of reincarnation in which children seem to remember details of a previous lifetime.

Astronomers now suggest that the visible universe may well have no observable beginning or end, but may twist back on itself in a way we cannot yet understand. Theories of a pulsating universe sound much like the early Hindu teaching of a universe that follows cycles. Physicists are explaining that one cannot really be certain whether or not a particle of matter exists. Mathematicians talk of shapes and structures that cannot be seen and could not exist in a world of only three dimensions.

Laboratory tests seem to have identified a kind

of unseen human energy that can move objects from a distance. New research indicates that some people possess the ability to heal animals or other human beings by touch. Indeed, there is little in modern science that is not just as miraculous as the stories in the early religious books.

Psychic Science

Through the ages certain beliefs have been called "occult," meaning *hidden*. While many useless superstitions have grown up around these beliefs, they should not be ignored. After all, most of the religious ideas about God, heaven, or an afterlife are also partly hidden.

Today many practical people are taking a fresh look at the occult. Some modern psychologists have introduced a science called parapsychology, the study of more than the usual faculties of the mind.

Serious testing is being done with subjects who sometimes have accurate knowledge of what is going on elsewhere through other than normal means. These people, like the prophets of old, seem to be able to predict the future with some degree of accuracy.

One of the most intriguing personalities being studied now is Edgar Cayce, who died in 1945. Cayce, when in a trance, seemed to have sources of knowledge far beyond those of his conscious mind. He was able to visualize accurately the bodies and illnesses of people whom he did not know and who lived far away. While the waking Cayce knew nothing about medicine, the sleeping Cayce spoke with the knowledge of a master physician and was able to prescribe many practical cures.

Cayce also was a storehouse of information about the past history and geology of the earth. He stated that many people have lived several lives before their present ones. He mentioned a continent named Lemuria in the Pacific Ocean, and made numerous references to another continent, Atlantis, in the Atlantic Ocean, which contained an advanced civilization. According to Cayce, the continent was

destroyed in widely separated stages, partly through
the misuse of energy by its inhabitants. In addition,
Cayce described people who lived at the time of
Zoroaster, furnished information about various Old
Testament prophets, and gave details about the
Essenes and Jesus. He suggests that Jesus traveled
to at least three foreign areas and received a complete religious education. According to Cayce, one
area was Persia, where Jesus learned about the Parsi
religion, another was India, where he studied Hinduism and Buddhism, and the third was Egypt, where
he became familiar with the best Egyptian training
for mastery of mind and body.

Much of Cayce's information did not agree with
accepted ideas about history. For example, Cayce
states that the great pyramid of Egypt, dated by
most historians about 300 years B.C., was actually
built much earlier around 10,000 B.C. by people
who included descendants of those from Atlantis.
This earlier pyramid is a marvel of precise construction, far better than those built later, and has
always been a mystery. When Cayce was alive
most people thought that Lemuria and Atlantis
were only legendary places. The Dead Sea Scrolls,

not found until several years after Cayce's death, were yet to reveal some of the important information about the Essenes that we know today. In many particulars Cayce was correct about the Essenes, although he never had studied this group. Recent evidence suggests that Cayce also may prove to be basically correct about Atlantis and other earth changes he has described.

Cayce predicted that land which was once a

Great pyramid of Gizeh,
masterpiece of precise
mathematical construction,
held an open tomb,
symbol of eternal life.

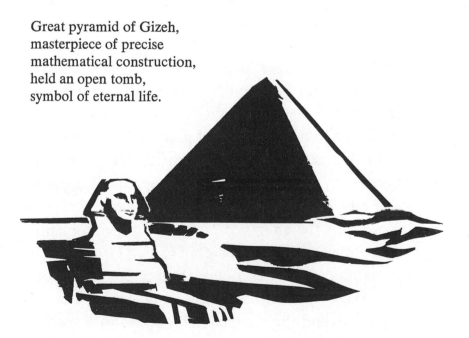

part of the continent of Atlantis would emerge
again around 1969. He said that a temple from
that sunken civilization probably would be redis-
covered along with records that had been preserved
in it. Off the coast of the island of Bimini, in the
area identified by Cayce, divers have located the
remains of a large temple submerged beneath the
water. Perhaps it may turn out that this temple did
belong to the vanished civilization of Atlantis.

An institute called the Edgar Cayce Foundation
has developed around the life work of this unusual
man. A few physicians, psychologists, geologists,
and historians have begun to study the material
collected about him and to relate it to present-day
discoveries. The results of this research may revise
our ideas about the history of man and his religions.

The Cayce research has spurred other similar
projects. In Princeton, New Jersey, the Religious
Research Foundation of America has pioneered
the study of the effects of prayer on growing plants.
For many years a gifted psychic named Grace Loehr
has worked with the Foundation much as Cayce
did. Like Cayce, Grace Loehr is able to tap information beyond the normal when she is in a trance.

Much of the information she has supplied relates to the nature of the soul. The research suggests that what is usually called the soul is quite complex. One "soul" may divide into two parts for earth experience or work together with other soul groups and units. An exciting possibility of this new research is that the information may help to explain the contrasting ideas about the soul that have appeared in various religious traditions.

On a more practical level, laboratory experiments have been conducted that deal with the measurement of this hidden part of human life. One hospital doctor placed the bed of each patient near death on an extremely delicate scale. The weight of the patient was noted regularly. Allowing for the loss of air from the lungs, a sudden additional drop in weight at the moment of death was registered in several cases, suggesting that some unseen substance had left the body.

A Russian husband-and-wife team of scientists, the Kirlians, have made an unusual breakthrough along similar lines. Using a special electrical device, they have been able to photograph an energy field in and around living objects. In one test, a third of a fresh leaf was cut away. The remaining part of the leaf then was photographed, using their special procedure. In the picture the missing section still was visible as an extension of the energy field. Such research supports the idea that there are other levels of life in addition to the ordinary physical. Of course, this concept is just what religion has tried to stress through the ages, so science and religion seem to be finding common ground.

New Archeology

New discoveries in archeology constantly are revising accounts of man's religious history. The Dead Sea Scrolls have brought to light some of the links between the Jewish and Christian traditions. Parts of the sunken city of Akhetaton in Egypt were dug out and brought to view once again. Also, with the use of a computer, thousands of decorated blocks from one of Ikhnaton's earlier temples at Karnak are being matched together again.

In the first half of this century, the minerologist

William Niven uncovered three layers of buried
city architecture in the vicinity of Mexico City,
the deepest find being some 25 feet below the surface. Although Mexico City is now located on a
plateau some 7000 feet high and is surrounded by
mountain ranges, these buried cities suggest that
the land was once near sea level. Each buried layer
is covered by stones and boulders, which to the
archeologist signifies that great floods or tidal waves
may have swept over the area. The artifacts found
in the deepest layer show that their makers were
skilled in crafts and metal working. Yet this civilization may have existed many thousands of years
before the Bronze Age. Such discoveries have called
into question accepted theories about the age of
mountains and changes in the surface of the earth.
They also demonstate that advanced civilizations
may have existed long before those we commonly
study.

New evaluations of the ruins found on more than
twenty South Pacific islands suggest that they may
have shared once the architecture of a single culture,
perhaps even that of Lemuria, or Mu, referred to
in many ancient records. James Churchward, a

colonel in the British Army and a lifelong amateur archeologist, proposed the theory that these islands are the remnants of a vast continent once located in the Pacific Ocean.

Churchward describes a map discovered in a Tibetan monastery, where he studied religion and ancient languages. Positions of constellations found on the map date the period it represents as about 25,000 years ago. Part of the map shows the area of the Amazon River and its swamp in South America as a lake extending across most of the continent. A short canal connects the lake to the Pacific Ocean. Churchward suggests that the broken remains of canal ditches, which can be seen today on top of the Andes Mountains in that area, once may have been part of the canal located at sea level. In addition, the map shows the tip of a large land mass in the Atlantic Ocean, located where the legendary Atlantis is believed to have existed.

Other ancient records point in the same direction. The historian Solon, who lived about 600 B.C., is quoted by Plato in a description of the size and location of Atlantis and an account of the sinking of the continent. Mention is made that large areas of the Atlantic Ocean were not safe for sailing vessels for a long time because of the existence of mud flats just beneath the surface.

Churchward, writing in the early 1930's, knew nothing of the statements of Edgar Cayce, which were not published until long after Cayce's death. Yet there are striking similarities in the information about Atlantis and Lemuria, including the suggested period, eleven or twelve thousand years ago, when Atlantis may have submerged finally.

Whether these lost continents once existed or not, evidence is appearing that early cultures shared certain religious beliefs and symbols. The interlocked triangles of the Jewish Star of David can be traced back to both sides of the globe. Probably they first represented the physical and spiritual worlds interlocked, each triangle standing for the principle of three in one—God creates one, one creates two, two creates three, and three produce all things. The same equal-sided triangle was used in each of the four sides of the ancient pyramid, believed to be a sacred shape. Still other eight-part symbols found in Central America resemble those of the later Buddhists. The historian A. L. Balsham has noted

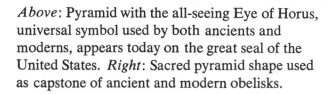

Above: Pyramid with the all-seeing Eye of Horus, universal symbol used by both ancients and moderns, appears today on the great seal of the United States. *Right*: Sacred pyramid shape used as capstone of ancient and modern obelisks.

that early inscriptions found in the Indus valley in India most resemble those still found today on the far distant Easter Island in the Pacific Ocean.

One theory proposed by Churchward and others is that the continent of Lemuria, or Mu, contained a civilization that became a great empire. Colonists from Mu may have brought elements of their religion and culture to the Far East. Later colonists from Atlantis may have spread a similar language and religion to areas of the Mediterranean Sea, including Greece and northern Egypt. If there was a water route across South America, it would have helped to make this ocean travel possible.

However, there is little agreement on the beginnings of man's religions. Much more study is needed before we reach a true understanding of our history, and recent discoveries indicate that an exciting period may be opening up in this investigation.

Experiments in Religion

The speed of modern transportation is enabling people of differing backgrounds to meet more often. The religious traditions from various parts of the world are mixing together. Thus, the familiar forms of worship, meditation, and ritual are changing. One may find a Catholic Church giving a seminar on Yoga or a Protestant group including jazz music in its service. There are churches and meditation groups organized entirely by young people.

Peace Corps workers traveling to the East have

come back to the United States with Hindu philosophical ideas. Hindus return to India with the
animation of Christian reformers. Churches of distinct denominations often are joining together as
community churches, ignoring the barriers of different beliefs or traditions that once kept them apart.
On the larger scale there are national ecumenical
movements in which Christians, Jews, and those
of other faiths attempt to come closer together in
worship and social services.

While many find fulfillment in this joining of
ideas, others are attempting to return to the original
essence of religious teachings. As archeologists and
historians help to cut away the debris of centuries,
people find it easier to understand and recapture
original religious beliefs. They are realizing that
although changes in custom and ritual have occurred, many basic principles still hold through the
centuries.

Perhaps more important than any of these trends
is the new freedom with which people of all ages
are turning to themselves for the answers to life's
mysteries. The renewed popularity of Yoga and
Zen are two among the more noticeable examples.

Thus, while religions have produced wise leaders and instructors, inspirational books, temples, prayers and rituals, perhaps each person is after all his own best source. Every man is his own prophet and the light of truth can be found within.

The one idea that all of the world's religions of past and present, East and West, seem to share is the power of universal love. Whatever the approach or the source, mankind is not likely to give up the search.

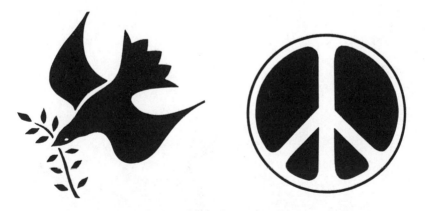

Left: Dove of peace with olive branch, symbol of return of life after the biblical flood. *Right*: Modern peace symbol, combining semaphore signal positions N and D for nuclear disarmament, also echoes shape of the foot of the dove in circle of unity.

Index

Indicates illustrations

About the Author

Larry Kettelkamp was born in Harvey, Illinois, and graduated from the University of Illinois, receiving a B.F.A. degree in painting in 1953. The following year he studied illustration at the Pratt Institute, Brooklyn, New York.

After two years' service as a lieutenant in the Army, Mr. Kettelkamp returned to Urbana, Illinois, where he joined the staff of Spencer Press as an artist in the curriculum department. He also has worked as a staff artist for the magazine *Highlights for Children* and as art supervisor for the Cranbury Elementary School, Cranbury, New Jersey. Now he devotes his time to writing, illustrating, and music composition. In addition, he frequently lectures on creativity, psychic research, and the preparation of text and illustration for children's books.

At present, Mr. Kettelkamp lives in Cranbury, New Jersey, with his wife and four children.